SYMPATHETIC BEASTS

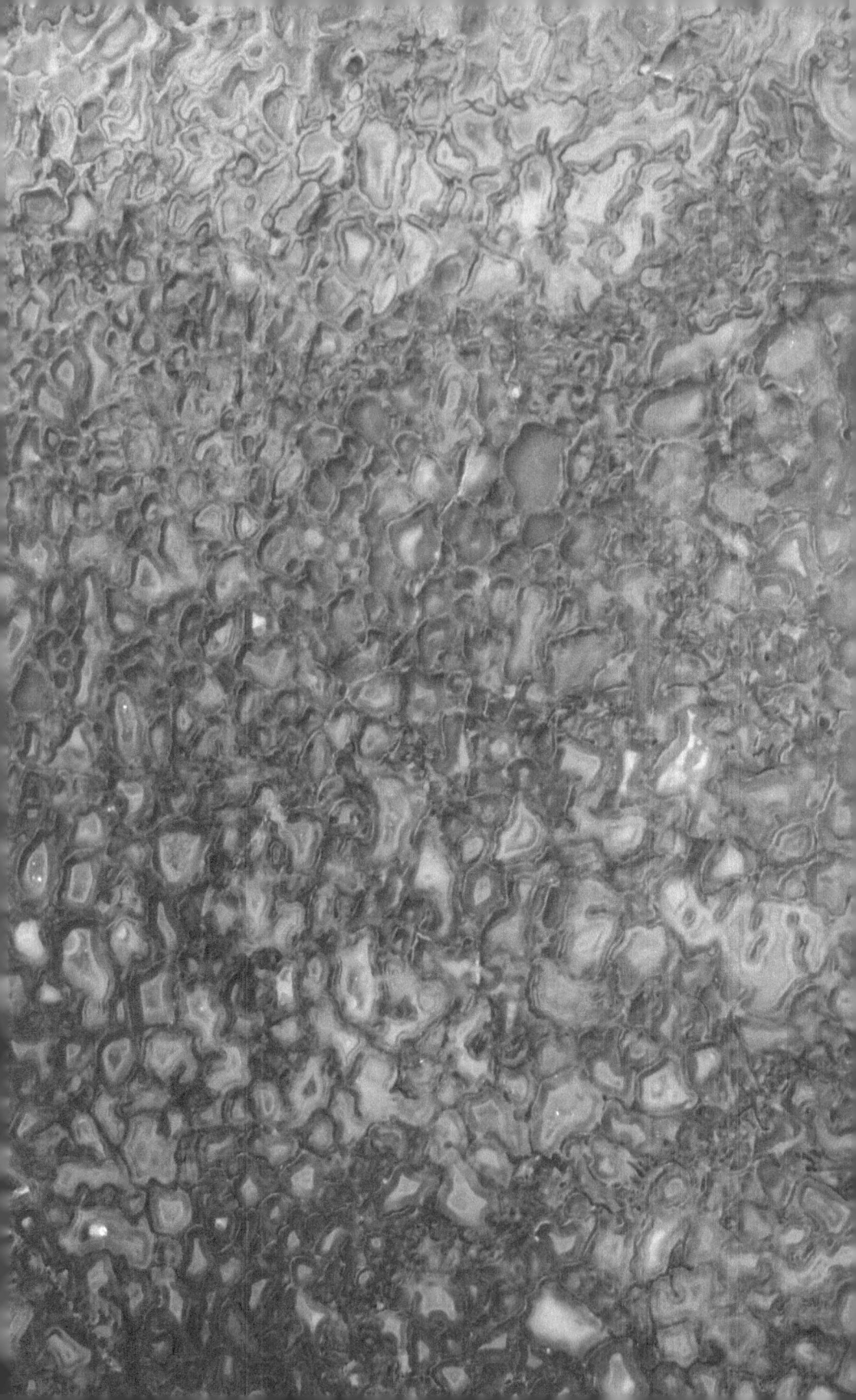

SYMPATHETIC BEASTS

Lucas Jacob

Published by
Next Page Press
San Antonio, Texas
www.nextpage-press.com
© 2023 Lucas Jacob. All rights reserved.

No part of this book may be used or reproduced in any manner without written permission from the publisher, except in context of reviews.

ISBN: 978-1-7366721-3-6
Library of Congress Control Number: 2022951481

Book team:
Laura Van Prooyen, Director and Editor
Cathlin Noonan, Associate Editor
Sheila Black, Associate Editor
Judy Jensen, Consultant
Tina Posner, Consultant
Amber Morena, Book Design

Cover Photo: Dinosaur Bone Cross Section
Photo Credit: istock "theotherdwayne"

for Madison

CONTENTS

ONE

Devotional   3
Objects in Mirror   4
The Wisdom of Hanna & Barbera   5
Not Going to the Beach   6
The Frog Prince of Wisconsin   7
Things that Are Too Easy   9
Two Views of Richard Serra's *Vortex*   10
Descent   12
Caution: Contents May Be   13
What Stays with Me   14
Stethoscopy   16
The Journey of the Glass Cobbler to the Palace   17
Hacksaw   19
Not for Use As   20
What I Tell Myself   21
Mystery   22
Declaring Victory   23
Capsized   24
Defense   26
Flotation Device Can Be Found   27
Voyeurism   28

TWO

The Theory of Deccan Volcanism   31

THREE

Sloe   46
Caution: Contents Under   47

Things that Can Break   48
On County H, Near Wabeno, Wisconsin   49
Keeping Time   50
Ceremony   51
Sanctuary   52
A Change in the Weather   53
The Body   54
Give Me   55
Fasten Safety Belt While   56
Audience   57
Kiss   58
Running   59
Matins   60
Desire Not Called by Its Name   61
The Royal She   62
Requiescat   63
The Dancer   64
Caution: Top Rung Not Meant   65
Swamp Walking   66
At the Neatline   67
Dry Spell   68
Child's Play   69
Roux   71
Tomorrow   72

Notes   73
Acknowledgments   75

SYMPATHETIC BEASTS

ONE

Devotional

Without once hatching a chick that would withstand
the fury of the Texas summer sun
or the blue jays that decorate the courtyard,
the same fat starling nests every year
in the bronze plastic planter hanging over
my balcony rail. Every May I am sure
that she will not come back, certain
that last year's hatchlings died before Easter,

as I remember cobwebs and desiccated
insect husks clinging to my fingers
when in winter I took the planter down
and lifted out the remnants of the nest.
Every May I am wrong about the timing
and about the persistence of the bird.
She returns and seems again to have built
her home overnight, reminding me

that I have not paid enough attention.
That days have gone by without my having
opened either the glass door or myself
to the morning air. That the will is not
a creature of fortune, but of habit.
It asserts itself not that it be honored,
particularly, come a spring morning
the color of a sun-bleached egg shell,

but that it at least be noticed, understood
as a bringer of song, a means for hearing
a note of hope when the spreading light
settles down to day and we are ready
to hear it, its gentle trill like the sound
of a water whistle blown against
the rising heat that would seem to threaten
any new life needing somewhere to begin.

Objects in Mirror

Are estranged from each other
and from you. Are reversed.
Somehow manage to keep
pace with the velocity
of memory. Are not
to be trusted, but are
in one sense reliable:
if you angle the glass just right,
you can see
how much closer
you are to yourself
than you at first appear.

The Wisdom of Hanna & Barbera

Scooby-Doo's creators knew nightmares
even better than pratfalls. How every wall
is false, sure to lead to the waiting arms
of the monster, leaving no barrier between
fear and the facing it. How you know your friends
are somewhere in a creaking, cobwebbed corridor
calling out your name, but you can't hear them.
Only your own echoing cry reaches your ears.

It's true: the villain is always the first
or the second of the strangers you meet
who offer to guide you through this new place.
The power outage is never just the storm.
Every rumor of danger in the shadows
is another reason to seek out the light.
Even the hallucinatory, madcap
chase scene, with its Rube Goldberg machine

is dead-on. Everything really does depend
on dime-store roller-skates, an oversized fan,
a wooden washtub, and glue fashioned
from nothing more than a stick of chewing-gum
and a surplus of unshakeable belief.
But more than anything else, they captured
the weightlessness through which panic becomes
a kind of peace. In my dream, for example,

there is a man I am required to kill,
my dawning terror not of the unknown,
but of knowledge itself. I know him well.
How comforting it is to find my feet
spinning harmlessly in the air, my quarry,
like any member of Scooby's amiable,
rag-tag gang, safely just beyond the reach
of my monstrous, unfamiliar hands.

Not Going to the Beach

Where a woman with a salt-spray voice
might have joined you leaning at the rail
along the boardwalk, asking for a glance
by asking your opinion on the weather
you were sharing.

Her long skirt pressed to her thighs by the wind
as if by immersion in your thoughts
of the water you both watched tugging,
in retreat, at seaweed and the edges
of misshapen hearts

drawn by teenage lovers at the tide line.
She'd have met your voice, foreign even
to you in the breeze, with a careless laugh
of invitation. The nerve of her, filling
your memories

of a trip you did not take, standing
in a brightness your face never felt,
casting a shadow that, not being there,
could not reach out toward your own, laughing
not to be heard, except
                        in your sun-starved mind.

The Frog Prince of Wisconsin

The ricochet of a doe back into the woods.
A doe he had surprised with steps crunching
along the side of the country road that he followed
carelessly with his thoughts and furtive flies,
dancing now at his cheeks, and then back out
into the air. The first sound was like a rifle report;
then came receding thrashings that would have meant
the shooter had missed his mark, had there been a shooter,
had the doe been the watched and not the watcher.
He saw only the flash of white as she turned tail,
and put him in mind of fairy stories in the woods,

of transformations of form, fur, and flesh,
tales of the troubling of waters, of loss among
enchanted trees. He walked on, each step on the rocks—
the surface was not gravel, really, but dusty clay
rife with fragments of silver-tipped rocks, their heads
like little whitecaps on the lake of the rust-red road—
each step grinding memory into fact: she was gone;
he was not; roads stretched on; there would be
no brushing of lips to bring out the royalty in his bloodline,
to bring him out into impossible teeth and hair
like spun fibers on the golden card of the loom

of an un-jealous god. When he strayed to the edge
of the road, trees filtered the sun's rays and diffused
his shadow, and this threw into question even
the absence of light he wrought on the ground,
because shade moving through shade is only
a matter of degrees of darkness. And so walking
he nearly passed by the flattened frog. Host of flies
turning lazy loops, it was well into whatever afterlife.
It had left its emptied skin behind in the middle
of the road. He stopped and bent to consider
this mournful little effigy hung between his eyes

and the clay, backlit, it seemed, by the summer-baked earth.
Here was the perfect backdrop for beholding
things ground down into elemental shapes, anything
suddenly stilled, anything arrested to a parody
of its former motion. The doe, by now, was deep
in the surrounding wood. He looked up and regarded
the tall, still grasses at the verge, in which branches
unsnapped sat silent, waiting. He stood, took a single,
stone-crunching step, and paused to marvel at it—
that he could disturb the morning at all, thinking,
This desiccated shell, this hollow husk I am become.

Things that Are Too Easy

Finding for yourself, just in time, a rhyme
with which to turn a phrase from maudlin back
toward cool and dry. Tying off. Losing track.
Winning a smile. Hedging. Dropping a dime

on the sister who has lifted your dress
or the brother who will never come down.
Ending the day with the kiss and yawn
that say *No dice, no sweat, and no caress.*

Giving a name to the place the mind goes,
all honey-on-tongue, all hung with a light,
airy refusal to wake up and fight.
Sounding its echo. And calling it No.

Two Views of Richard Serra's *Vortex*

at the Modern Art Museum, Fort Worth, TX

I. Approaching from the parking lot

The cars squat before it,
all their colors
gone to white in the glare
of our looking up.
A swish of motion
on the boulevard.
We are stilled but humming,
holding distance enough.

I train my eyes on the slit
where two massive plates
part below their overlapping
to allow the curious
to step inside. Like a skirt
designed to frame the thigh.
I walk toward that which today
I will leave untouched.

II. Looking back from the sculpture garden on the roof

An unmoving tree like a fan
held before the face
of a blushing god.
At its darkest, your hair
is the color of Cor-Ten steel
on a cloud-stone afternoon.
The machine fans hush the city.
I look back. Vortex

stands ballerina-straight.
Where the blue cuts the clouds
the open mouth at the top
of Serra's work sucks strips
of plaster from the sky.
I am glad to have this
absence. No need to find
another one in your eyes.

Descent

In search of a place that was exempt
from poetry, she set out as you might expect:

from the top of a steep-backed flight
of uneven wooden stairs, themselves

hidden behind a cellar door padlocked
against use even by the inhabitants

of the house. She set her mind
to darkness, and thereby found the key,

hung from a nail aslant an angular
shadow in the pantry. The obvious place.

Prepared, then, to be literal,
she began the descent. The flick

of a switch provided her with curled
ribbons of light, as if from a bulb

latticed with wire. She shrugged off
webs and let the mossy tang of mold

cling in her nostrils. When she took
the last step, and heard unmuffled her own

bare footfall, a slap of flesh on stone,
she thought there must be some mistake.

But though she cast herself willingly
into the black gauze of what looked

to be boundless space, she could not
leave behind such sounds: her feet

shuffling through dust, the sloshing
of the blood, unstilled, in her veins.

Caution: Contents May Be

Exactly what you asked for, and who wants
a cup of confirmed expectations? No,
it's better by far to be taken by
the scruff of the neck, dragged into the light,
and left there in the glare of naked truth.

Who'd have thought that such a simple request
for a kick-start to the day would have led
right past wish, to desire? And who needs,
let alone wants, any one or thing
that is not achingly, steaming-in-your-face,
fogging-up-your-lenses, put-me-down, hot?

What Stays with Me

Jane's face rising like smoke
on the surface of a blackened
car window. Someone saying

something was holy.
Unexpected. Or more likely

saying something wholly
profane—like holy hell, man
look, will you? Look

at that thing burn. We did,
impressed enough to forget

to be unimpressed. A glance
flickered from one to another
of us, diminished by each

passing-on until it was barely
more than an aversion of the eyes.

This is how, at middle age
in an airport, on a holiday,
under blue lights too diffuse

to cast shadows around the forms
moving through well-ordered space,

I can watch the bodies
of the other travelers without
myself being watched. A trick

learned in adolescence: to see
something by not looking at it.

Whoever said whatever was
or was not sacred perhaps no longer
remembers it—if I who so wish

to do so cannot. But Jane is less
a ghost now than she was then,

when her features stretched across glass
darkened by the lightless place
we had found. What we wanted I want

to remember, but suspect
that it was just not to be alone.

Together we made the sense
that we were together, a sense
like a patchwork kite designed

for night flying, so that we could
feel its ascent in our wrists,

its buoyant dance up and beyond
what we knew of a fragile string
trailing away into darkness.

So long as it holds, even
the flimsiest of frames

can carry aloft and sustain there
in the breeze wishes wished
just hard enough to take flight.

Stethoscopy

Everything has a twin, she said.
The rebar exposed where concrete
has surrendered to the weather
has its shadow, elongated
like the minute hand on a sundial
without a face. The dogs in the park
grow tired chasing themselves
at the tail in grasses tall enough
for the blades to have split halfway up.

And you and I? She smiled
as at a memory of drawing
hopscotch squares, as if the question
took her back to the thick green chalk
whose dust filled with a sweaty paste
every crease in the skin of every finger.

We have what we see in each other,
she said. What we see as each other.
She meant not to get too close,
I supposed, as her step took on
a new cadence, each footfall
timed to sound out an echo of mine,
like the closings of two valves.

The Journey of the Glass Cobbler to the Palace

I.

She half-watched the shadow of the carriage, too distracted by her errand to mistake it for birds or any other creatures of the woods. A summons from the prince was, her father had taught her, good for the coffers, if not for the nerves.

He'd left her his wisdom and the secrets of his trade: how to spin glass into baubles for those who could afford breakable things—tear-drop pendants, icicle window chimes, crystal shoes for husk-and-rag dolls made by the seamstress whose tidy home sat in the same row of artisans' huts.

She imagined being shown a portrait of the late queen. The prince would ask her to capture mother's eyes for a string of beads. Or he'd plop the dog of the court stinking in her lap: she'd be told to fashion a collar that would reflect all the candles in the great chandelier hanging like a constellation over her head.

It never occurred to her that she'd be asked to make a mate for a girl's slipper, for the prince to carry from door to door.

II.

He told her, as if explaining that rain came mostly on cloudy days, that of course he must have the matched set. What if the shoe retained by the fleeing child, so charmingly disarmed at the witching hour, should have cracked in that flight?

If she had known, at least she could have spread the word throughout the neighborhood to be out of the house when the prince brought his new fetish to town.

As it was, she was kept at the palace until her work was done.

Back home, she did her best not to hear the end of the tale from which she expected to be erased. She knew that happily and had imagined that ever after.

She continued to make fragile, light-filled things, her hands steady as ever. She knew the breaking could always come later.

Hacksaw

The way he looked at you.

Said, what are you
busy about, buzzing
through these halls,
causing no end
of shaking along the walls?

Said, here's a heavy load—
has to be halved
somehow, some way, so
how's about it? His half
here, hers there.

Said, shouldn't shake
just to see a man
shoulder the shaggy
burden he shares
only with himself.

Said, there's no thing
standing so thick
in this world
these teeth
can't cut through it.

Not for Use As

Often as you might like. A telescope,
for example, tends to wait in a closet
for the Leonids or the Perseids,
only to stay there when the spreading pool
of city glow swallows the sky, its light
show now the only game in town. It is
like water, this undulating un-night
that sluices off of shingles and shimmers
on the leaded glass behind which dozes
the next day's news. Which car plying these waves
carries anything, however modest,
that might serve as a flotation device?

What I Tell Myself

There's more of you
to love
when we are not
together.

Alone
you are you
and you
alone.
Not you
and you
and you.

So hold yourself
to you
and I will
mine
to me.

To be
together
alone
is almost
to be
alone together.

Mystery

for Madison

I think I know who did it.
I hit "pause" and silence the room.
You roll your voice and play along:
Okay, who?
The killer. Having known this
was coming, you don't dignify it
even with an "mmm-hmm."

You release the image
back into motion. We press
our shoulders together, our gaze
still on the screen.

This is love.
Anyone outside will see
whatever a silhouette shows,
and know nothing
of the language
two people create together.

Declaring Victory

Thirteen times I went to the edge
of the water. Every day
for nearly two weeks. The egrets
stood indifferent to my comings
and unaware of my goings.

Once I took a photo of a lone
sunflower on the bank, not knowing
of a field of them just downstream.

Had I known, I might have gone
so far as to have snapped
one of the stalks down low enough
to obscure the fact of the theft,
the flower field being hard against
a one-strand wire fence. As it was,
I let the photo be the stem
and blooming of my wishes.

That I stay true to this new resolve.
That the river run high enough
to move the angular white birds
onto larger stones. That the one
in thought give way to the two
in a field of words, their sound
a rushing like wind past thick stalks,
or the flapping of outstretched wings.

Capsized

I. *Bridgman, Michigan—with Andrew and Jason*

The Sunfish went over, and we went too,
falling without effort into cool water.
Michigan: lines of dune behind,
green swells and seagull chatter.
An ashen sky clouded the lake.
We bobbed like buoys, laughing at our luck

and at ourselves, convinced we'd survive
in awkward life vests, the shore within view.
We'd have a fire on the beach, ash floating
over the surf, and among us a vow
for the next fire night: girls by our sides
filling the slight depressions in the sand,

soft hair touched by flickering light.
We were nineteen, so easy in our dreams,
easy in that water with the capsized boat.
The swells thumped against fiberglass like drum-
beats; Jason clung, smiling, to the hull;
Andrew gathered flotsam for the long haul

back to shore: centerboard, broken rudder.
Nineteen, we did not think once of drowning.
We reached the beach, shared a sheepish laugh,
and left the lot on the hot sand, draining.
In an apple glow Michigan sunset
we had our fire, alone where we sat.

II. *Ten years later, Boston—with Andrew and Cathy, Jason and Liz*

North to see Andrew thrown over again.
It was love this time, no simple lake's wave.
The Boston skyline, Jason in a sleek
car by night—a fantasy of his wife's,
he said, clinging to his smile. Fresh snow
in drifts, suburban driveways, all that was new

at twenty-nine: a love seat, and irises,
their stems refracted by leaded glass,
on a sturdy tiled table. Andrew came,
shook off snow in the transom. The flakes glistened
briefly on the mat and were gone. Falling
into a grown-up chair in a room full

of friends from dogeared postcard summers,
he said Cathy was swimming, would come straight
from the pool. I pictured her wet hair
and raw red nose. The Michigan beach strut
of a teenage girl on the sand. A decade—
days of glass, years like fallen ash—to decide

the dreams of adolescence. Or so it seemed.
She came at last: not some girl of a summer
mirage, but a woman warming winter.
No space in Andrew's chair, all the same
she fell in beside him without effort.
He sank there smiling and put up no fight.

Defense

No one attends the weather-warped
display counter of what was a newsstand
on the corner. The wares arrayed there—
a paperweight cityscape from before the fall,
an ivoried Madonna cradling the space
emptied of the child, and four volumes thick
with moisture-bloated pages ever expanding—
can be purchased at any time
by anyone credulous enough to slap
his fear down like currency on the wood.

Yes, it is a he, nearly every time.
The furtive approach, after many
passings-by as if by chance. The sidelong glance.
A watcher at any of the grimy windows
that moan in the winds of this place
will sense the shudder not quite buried
by the shabby overcoat. The frisson
of feeling himself in danger. A grainy
black-and-white projection of the limited
imagination of the confidence man.

Flotation Device Can Be Found

Just behind your back, or just beyond
that shabby curtain. Of course, any
situation in which you need to find it
will be one in which you lose it.
The irony is sharp like the teeth
of the shadowy swimmers you feel
but can't see when you sleep. Those elegant
surrogates that glide through the waters
of your fears, all silent displacements
and unwelcome waves, so much easier
to name than whatever lurks much closer
at hand, perhaps right there beneath your seat.

Voyeurism

Fireflies like buoy lights
ride the waves of falling night
with the flotsam of the day.
A low limb stirs shadowed hints
of objects around the trees.
We see twinned heads bobbing
in and out of view amid strips
of blue cast through window blinds
onto the green.

                Their rising
and falling mark a horizon
ruffled by currents of air
and color, sweet summer rot
of the trees' syrup smell.

We cast our glances away
and remember shame.
Though soon they drift back,
guided by our giving in
to memories of nights together,
apart, searching out shadows
we hoped would hide
what we'd found—brightest
if briefest flicker in the dark.

TWO

Dinosaurs are what paleontologists call "charismatic megafauna": sexy, sympathetic beasts whose obliteration transfixes . . . anyone with a pulse. The nature of their downfall . . . might offer clues for how we can prevent, or at least delay, our own end.

—BIANCA BOSKER, IN *THE ATLANTIC*

The Theory of Deccan Volcanism

Which holds that the Cretaceous-Tertiary extinction was caused not by an asteroid, but by thousands of years' worth of volcanic eruptions in the Deccan Plateau of what is now India.

The textbooks say an asteroid did it. A flash like the simultaneous illumination of all of the nightlights ever switched on in the long history of waiting, and the dying began.

The Deccan Volcanists disagree.

They are like a punk band with too long a name, and just the right length of sneer. Asteroid, indeed. As if one big space rock could roll back hundreds of millions of years of life stubborn as gravity.

The volcanoes scattered the ashes of millennia. The lowering sky met the scalded, pockmarked land. The kind of ending you can believe in, relentless and unafraid to tell it like it is, again and again, until everyone is listening.

Who wouldn't want to be a sexy beast? So the price is a long goodbye and the uninvited pity of a clay-faced successor to the throne. The one can't be helped; the other is millions of years down the carbon-dark road. Enjoy the beginning of the end. Stretch that long, curved neck out toward the still undiminished light of the sun.

We imagine the end of our world in the fall of CGI monuments. The authoritative roar of Dolby SurroundSound. Always, somehow, some of the faithful are saved.

What would Sue the T. Rex think of us if she knew that we refuse to press "pause" on our Armageddon?

Or that we still haven't figured out what she did with the twiglike hands she could not raise high enough to wipe the accumulating ash from her eyes?

Of course, the asteroid has its attractions. That giant hole in the Yucatàn: a one-hundred-and-eleven-mile concavity shaped to cradle the biggest of ideas. To shush the tremulous cries that would splash up and over the walls of any smaller vessel.

O shelter us from thy relentless changes, Earth our Protector. Deliver us not into the fullness of knowledge. Thy indifference repels. Let us know not the smoke and liquid flame, nor the whispered breath of air on which is fed the fire.

It must have been a one-off. So unlikely that a new calculus is needed to determine the odds of an encore. The Book is sealed that rests upon the altar of Geology. Why break that bond and read the words we dare not speak aloud into the silence we have made a hole in our fears?

The Deccan Volcanists lock their doors at night, just like the rest of us. They, too, mistrust any darkness, however small, that eludes the city's surfeit of low-pressure-sodium bulbs.

Forces gather there. In recessed doorways. Under overburdened summer trees. The Volcanists draw their blinds without a glance, if not without a thought.

They settle into repose, complaining of creaking joints. Bouncing a foot once, twice, and again, so as to raise it high enough to grasp a shoe or sock. The setting differs only in the sense of humor displayed with pride on the bedside table.

A lava lamp, switched on to accompany the brushing of teeth, the reading of a murder mystery. Switched off again with a chiding. As the pulsing blotches recede from the walls, a voice in the blackness that could belong to any of us: *Oh, no, you don't, my love. The world doesn't end tonight.*

But their heightened senses in half-sleep betray them. They are different.

They hear the sloshing of the molten core. Feel the heat through the sheets, mattress, floor, foundation. Taste the iron by touching tongue to hard palate.

They close their eyes, only to see tectonic plates colliding. Where we are weightless in our falling, they are grave. Aware of the descent. Counting layers of consciousness like striations in exposed rock.

Knowing what the rock once was, and will be again.

I'd like to think like a Deccan Volcanist, my insight on the outside of the accepted wisdom. I would disavow asteroids and comets—all manner of celestial leftovers from when a mere solar nebula collapsed upon itself and became our solar system.

While I was at it, I'd have a thing or two to say about memory, love, longing, and hope.

Anything whose orbit might bring it just a bit too close for comfort.

My gaze wanders into the middle distance.

Buildings like a bar graph. The page an acid-free pale afternoon sky.

I lack the patience necessary to brush the dust from these bones.

It was a spike in iridium levels that led the asteroid fetishists to their so-called Crater of Doom. A nice touch, that. Neither self-serious nor easily ignored. A sweet spot in the art of naming.

Or the writing of epitaphs.

How will ours read when it's all said and done and we have burned everything that will take to flame? *Here lies the dream of the eternal, may it rest at last?*

We call them fossil fuels. As if it's what they're made of, not what they will make of us. We make of ourselves monuments in glass and chrome, and line the vaults below with whatever currency. Salt. Bone. Drachma or shilling. Pelt or hide. Krugerrand or skull.

We must remember, always, the necessary cut-outs. An impressive door through which to enter. A hole through which to breathe.

Many of the species that made it through the Cretaceous-Tertiary extinction lived below the surface.

The kinds of dens we draw in cross-section in children's books, ready to be turned around and held up for any number of bedtime readings. Doilies on the arms of little chairs. Grandfather clocks in miniature. In the family portrait on the wall of packed earth, everyone standing erect.

A dining table, well laid, in the foreground.

Nothing to tell us what it is—or who—that threatens the world just beyond the edge of the page.

When the groaning machines of pre-dawn sweep the streets toward daybreak, the Volcanists arise and feel magnanimous in their waking.

Either way, it was a hell of a show.

The most determined chain reaction of splitting atoms climaxes like a pop-gun by comparison. The volcanoes of the Deccan Pleateau beggar any mythology of fire; the asteroid any metaphor for change.

Either way, we still have those impossible bones from which to build the creatures that populate the landscapes of the imagination.

It might just as well have been both.

The glossy sheen in the wake of the rotating brushes. So many window shades lit up from behind, one after another. Alone, each is merely plausible. Together they define the start of what we call the day.

How it will end is not the morning's concern.

It will.

The city will come around again into shadow. The sodium lights will blink into life. Cars drained of some portion of the fuel that fired them in their leaving will scurry back behind doors that rise and fall at the touch of a button. The buttons will hum with the battery life that can be felt only by those who hold still enough for long enough.

For now, the Volcanists greet the dawn and re-commit themselves to their work.

Knowing once again and for certain that every dying out, no matter how abrupt it seems, has been a conclusion foretold, if not foregone.

THREE

Sloe

To my ear, it always sounded
like not-fast gin, as if
by virtue of a somehow casual
fermentation, the stuff would
creep up on you, thickening
your thoughts and tongue
before you knew what hit you.

How delicious to know now
that the sour fruit
of *prunus spinosa* is called
a drupe, and does exactly that
in blackthorn bunches, hanging
in tight-knit clumps like organs
drawn in against needing
a quick one for the road.

Caution: Contents Under

Review, which means we could be talking
about a hell of a long delay.
Seems that every time there's a bang-bang play,
it's back to the super-slo-mo. We want
to get it right, they say. Well, sure, we all do,
but mostly we don't. An errant word,

a slip of paper recycled unread,
apologies unheard because unsaid.
Shadows stretch to meet just where intentions
fall away. The angle is all wrong.
Ten times out of ten the trick is played.
The eye is an imperfect instrument,
easily fooled and governed by pressure.

Things that Can Break

The vow you made about your songbirds, how
you'd always keep the pair together, close
enough to wish if not to touch, which goes
to show just who and where we are right now.

The fever that brings technicolor dreams
in which I'd gladly stay if staying were
a choice to make, like choosing to taste your
new flavor just because it is new. Seams

at which we pull as if to test their truth.
Dawn. News of dawn. A storm at dawn throwing
rain like pebbles at the glass, our knowing
that we alone are belief in need of proof.

On County H, Near Wabeno, Wisconsin

The road to the south twisted like the stream
in an amateur landscape, trying too hard
to look unplanned. It was difficult there
to reconcile the unbranching trunks
on the hill with the carpet of plaited green
laid out below. I got out of the car, jumped
onto the hood, walked over the windshield

up to the roof. I felt I ought to have held
a fine-winged creature cupped in my hand,
so I behaved as though I did: released
a breath into motionless air, eased my arm
away from my body, and uncurled
each finger in turn. Even melodrama
can be an act of faith. The silence stretched.

Neither the pine wood around the car nor
the field beyond the foot of the hill was changed
by this performance. My palm opened empty
to the sky and the meandering road.
But the feathered shadow I could not have cast
from the driver's seat flew up to meet me
as I returned with a leap to the ground.

Keeping Time

Like an afterthought at the edge
of your hearing, her footfall
made you wonder how such a sound
could contain even a touch
of personality, the barest hint
of someone worth remembering.

The day held its light. The night
at bay, you marveled at how
the heart's rhythm is heard
only when there is around us
some mimicry of its beating:

a clock's tock sounding the depths
of an unfamiliar room; cicadas
scratching at dusk; this walking away
over dry stones; the breaths we count
alone in any breathless hour.

Ceremony

for Ashley and Marshall

"We'll hold a feast in great solemnity"
—*A Midsummer Night's Dream*, Act IV, scene 1

How much words change. The years pass.
Connotation turns ears of wheat
to ash. We think of mourning,
of final prayers carved into stone.
Of those comings-together
reserved for the darkest of our tears.

By now, you both have shed your share
of skins, left behind the residue
of days too long and nights too full
with talk of loss and what it takes.
Ready, then, to add another
reed-thin voice to the choir singing

of what is to come, you'd rather weep
to hear that sound: of a music
as yet untuned but growing
into its notes. Such delicate work,
like hands in a lilac breeze pulling
in close the threads of kinship.
Let us name this new bond in old words
fitted to the occasion, and hold
your solemn feast in reverence
for how meanings shift, how people
go when we wish that they could stay,
and how others come to us in time.

Sanctuary

A black box. A cube sized neither for height
nor for width, but for volume. For the air
needed to sustain the stubborn candle
whose wick will not concede to tallow
any measure of its braided length.

The box admits no witness to the pageant
thus contained. This striptease where the body
is just another garment to be shed.

No music urges the flame's dancing
to a tempo other than its own rhythm
of sighs. What pools inside the box assumes
a form described by four walls. Symmetry
pretends at meaning. The little fire
whose light is faith burns jagged just the same.

A Change in the Weather

Everything dried out: his carpet,
dampened by a rain that had come
and gone before he'd recognized
that the sound against the screen
was more than the rattle of wind
he'd listened to for uncounted hours;

the skin on the backs of his hands,
rubbed nearly red and now free
of the sweat he'd found there when last
he'd acknowledged his body;
the air that had been a blanket draped
over the day. So this was how

quickly the waters parted,
how easily the blood turned to dust.
In the arid night, it was all
backward: the tides awaited the call
of the sun, the clouds shrank in the soft
waxen light of the cold waning moon.

The Body

All of your work, each fullness
you have wrung from the slimmest glimmer
of a notion—the comfort you found
in a head shaped like an apple,
like an old friend's, the longing
you heard in the merest whisper
of your hand's sliding across a sheet
of unlined paper, the miracle
of joy you found with that hand
and hers and the space between them—

this is the body. The one you can
give to her to read that needs neither
light nor voice. The one she can touch,
folding it back at the edges,
as you would curl into your desire
and quiver unsprung if she touched
the other. This is the body
in which you would live if you could—
the one you were not given, but made.

Give Me

The word for
five children jumping
in one square of cement.
A laugh that strayed so,
like a soft turning
in the hips.
A lover watching
five laughing children clutter
a sidewalk square in the rain.

Give me such a word, I'll open it
like a wildflower.
Insert it in the skin of the earth,
or string it like a bow, and shoot
myself into the clouds.
Spell it out across the sky.

Fasten Safety Belt While

You still can. One of these days, the damned thing
will fasten you. Will hold you rapt,
pun intended, while all the instruments
of tomorrow tell you in a chorus
of humanized voices that they really
meant today. It's you that will be in need
of a warning light. A pleasantly green,
distinctly analog indicator,
blinking out from behind your eyes the news
that although you are for the moment, you
will not for much longer remain seated.

Audience

> ". . . a chimera in my brain . . . troubles me in my prayer"
> —John Donne

A streak of whiteness mars the stage each time
the lights go out. It looks for all the world
like someone left a scrap of flesh behind

to mark the spot. We have to look. The crime
we've blinked away comes back. The curtain curls.
That streak of whiteness owns the stage. We time

our gasps for full effect. A blackout's fine
if it holds its peace—as if fog unfurled
and someone left. A scrap of flesh behind

the nails not sought will not be found. Each rhyme's
another pithy epithet to hurl,
to splash in white across the stage each time

the play rings true. And so we stand in line
to claim our seats again. *Give it a whirl!*
A scrap of fabric, that fleshy behind!

We say, "A darkness falls. The stars align,"
and worship not obsidian, but pearl.
A milky whiteness staged to sell. Sometimes,
a scrap of prayer: *to leave the flesh behind.*

Kiss

What the tires do to the curb
when I drop you off
outside the building. What you do
to the tips of your uncurled fingers
now that you are not beside me,
clutching at the straps of your bag.
I release one breath and pull away.

With *off* you scatter dandelion seeds,
a mere flick of your freckled wrist
to show me how you said goodbye
to someone whose name you've never mentioned
my never mentioning. *Up* is what you call me
when I say you're better left alone
if the summer scent you bring into a room
was not enough to hold him fast.
It's a dance we know well.

I tell you that I have seen
figures in sandalwood so fierce
that in silhouette they fill any aperture,
carved so that the maker's hands
not be idle. That woodwinds play
so breath has voice. That canvases stretch
to be touched with color.
That I return to you your words
simply to give my lips
something to do.

Running

on the Trinity Trail, just above the Benbrook Dam, Fort Worth, TX

The water is running sluggishly toward
the iron grating at your feet as you cross
the spillway, as if each bubble released
were just a small clearing of the throat.
The time for this indulgence is running out,
the sun at your left shoulder in the mirror
of the river as this day turns toward the next.
The Temptations' imagination, one thought
in six vocal parts, is running away from them,
running away from you, behind on your plan
to have a plan, running along as you were told to do
so many times when cornflower blue skies
sank to dusk and found you out here once again,
aware of the play of the breezes among
the river grasses, running into trouble as you tried
to rein it back in, this feeling that you
ought to turn the music down, ought to breathe
in deeply the drifting scent of rose blush
and cedar dust, ought to set aside *ought to*
and let yourself be, for once, not running
but walking, if alone, at least paired
with a shadow you don't mind watching
as it rises and falls along every fence
and wall you cannot climb toward home.

Matins

The insistence
of the starling sticks in the ear
much as the eye, struck by
the motion, so like intent,
of the branches just in bloom
waving in concert,
works to find a point of focus
along any one of the stark lines
not yet in green, or even
pale yellow, bud.

          Failing that,
the way the tree seems to stack
light upon light in layers
of dawn.

          Anything to dispel
what's left of the mist, the ache—
the mind addled by memory,
able to hear refrains but not
inventions, playing and re-playing
a birdsong like prayer.

Desire Not Called by Its Name

Pink and edged with dew,
each hyacinth, like the evidence
of an uncoupling, seems poised
to rejoin the scent it has given
to the air into which it breathes.

Loss may be so temporary
as not even to deserve
the word. Sometimes we want
to call back to us someone
who has not left, who is standing
right there, the curves
at her hips like smiles
on faces tilted just so.

There is no way to know
what the flowers know
of opening. All that remains
is to ask if, having come,
it might be nice not to have to go.

The Royal She

There was no shame in the old tales
in not living happily through the ever after.
They just never had to tell you that part,
taking it for granted as a figure of speech,

as one might understand that to give one's hand
need not be a bloody task, for all that it is
an amputation. The sun came up through trees
like stencils, the grass held pearls of dew

on every blade, and the beloved did not
know herself still to be so, so long
ago were her days and nights of being
held like a belief. But she felt no need

to ask her glass or her charming prince
of the workaday world. She read her shadow
every time she went to the well and pulled
it out of the depths with the bucket of water

skimmed with moss and the slime of pale blond stones.
She read it aloud, its contours forming
a delicate script on the muddied earth
at the well head. Seeing the shape of the light

her figure forbade, she'd smile to think that she
was happy, though not afraid not to be so,
if only because she carried herself
and knew she need not carry another's.

Requiescat

T.W., late of Dallas and Fort Worth

The golden hour. Gentle enough
to test a man's faith in any
light meter that favors instead
a moment not washed just so
in yellow-gone-to-blue. Less
a color; more a highlighting
of dust and small hairs. A granting
of nobility to old wounds.

You—whose films were shot only
in memory, flashing curves
of delicate muscle stretched out
to be touched by the digits
of desire in your gaze—you spoke
of it often, and told me
what it showed you of darkness.
Is it all darkness now? It is

enough so that we cannot talk
any more of silhouettes
like amber-shadow ghosts. You were
my friend before you were not.
When you took your life, you took
as well those moving pictures
that revealed old scars, if only
in golden moments once so prized.

The Dancer

Is a body
      among other bodies only I can see.
In silhouette she is black and stark
      against the Harlequins and Columbines
who try to overrun the stage.

They are gaudy
      in the colors of memory:
reds and yellows and flashes
      of silver.
They twirl around the dancer
as if she were a marker
      on the floor,
a stationary X, rather than the graceful
embodied motion she is.

I have a mind to know her
choreography, to understand
what I'm seeing as I sit
      on the edge of a second-row seat,
straining my eyes
      in the dark,
waiting for the low cloud of resin
kicked up
      in her wake
to settle, with my heart,
stilled
      at her feet.

Caution: Top Rung Not Meant

Which suggests that it is accidental,
a step never meant to be there at all,
which of course is the very best kind. Like
the one you take without a shoe despite
your sock's thin ribbing, just to know the snow
underfoot as if touching it with your hand.
Like the one not strictly in time that pulls
you in, that much closer. Like the one
that finds only air, an element
well suited for carrying scent, but not
weight, better for falling than for climbing.

Swamp Walking

We stepped where we could, on bunched tufts of growth.
The farther we went, the softer the ground.
Of course we should stop—should turn back around—
but frogs called and dusk fell. Perhaps we both

needed to know. I tried to understand
the way you moved, the way you balanced your
arms to stay out of the muck, how before
each step you reached back almost to my hand.

Finally, you gave up and plunged right in.
Sharing an embarrassed smile, the mud
between our toes, the quiver in the blood,
I followed you, my shoes soon in ruins.

It's obvious now what we didn't say yet:
sometimes it's enough just to get your feet wet.

At the Neatline

It takes a fool to build himself a keep
where defenses are not needed, proclaim
his own admiration for the thing,
and demand yours, too. But, then, fools
abound. The wisest court cartographers

always drew their borders with deep rivers,
and did not bother to tell the king,
whose endlessly drumming fingers
left an oily sheen on the drafting desk,
how every territory changes

just a little bit every day, how both banks
are eroded, such that some portion
of what seems so clearly defined will be
washed away in any given moment,
neither bank really a side at all,

just a temporary glimpse of a larger
un-making, the progress of every marker
to the sea, reminding us that everything
we claim is in fact mapped only on to
a paper-thin wish not to have to change.

Dry Spell

I will admit
    I want the lashings
        of rain, so rare in this place
to come not for the grass
    gone to tinder, but for me
        to be kept out of relentless

light. I am not proud
    of this wish to cloud
        the issue, especially in such
an obvious way. Better to focus
    on the rocks, usually just white-edged
        "V"s scattered across the Trinity,

and now bald heads resting
    on the shoulders of grasses
        that have found purchase
in the dry river's bed. Or
    on the strips of light that, finding
        me in mine, reveal too much

lately of the faded-rust walls,
    or on the thin film of silver
        unbrushed from the mirror,
or the pink imprint left
    on my skin by wrinkles in cotton
        bedclothes undisturbed overnight.

Child's Play

for Katy and for Gabe

I.

Webs of moisture at the screen,
a window open just enough
for a smell of mist and dampened bark,
and magic words:
    let's say
we're on a mountain,
or elsewhere in a wood. We played roles
adventuresome or domestic
all grown up
in a made world.
Saturdays, spring or fall,
with butter-topped muffins baking downstairs;
or any day in the summer,
with the hum of a window fan
from the back of the house
despite the rainy weather.

A made world was remade simply.
We'd climb down from the twin-bed mountain
to the carpeted floor
of my big-brother room:
    let's say
a ball field, the players dolls
and stuffed toys in endless rotation.
When sunshine returned, and voices
called from the drying pavement
or from the lacquered maple table,
the heart of the house,
we would simply pause.
The game would never end,
was neither won nor lost.

II.

Now, Saturdays in autumn
we play our games apart,
despite all those still unfinished
behind the screen
of memory.
     Let's say
a big brother still
makes rules to suit the moment:
today, in rain or sun,
this will be your city.
I say that it will,
just as, in a childhood room
with music from a plastic box,
I pretended at advice,
or led the game to my advantage.
Now it is to yours.

Pretending at advice.
How to make a marriage?
In the end, it's child's play:
     let's say
Katy will be a wife, and Gabe
will be her husband.
Play the game together
all grown up
with magic words.
Abide by ever-changing rules,
and welcome every rain
that demands you hunker down,
open wide your eyes
like children,
and make a brand-new world.

Roux

From the French,
and so r-o-u-x, not
an Old English name
for misgiving, though
it would be nice
to be able to roux
the day,
smoothing it out
as it darkens.

Tomorrow

Tomorrow I will give my enemy
these words of peace:
        you are welcome
    to the old animosities. May they
brighten your day with a darkness
unexpected and, therefore,
as sweet as new fruit.
        I am well. Come,
    sit with me and drink
in the silence the heart's
beating leaves when the blood
is kept inside.

I have missed you, I will say,
have missed my chance at you:
        I told a barefaced
    lie when I said I did not
need you. We all need desires
we do not understand, need the scent
of apple, a wish to taste
        the skin bare. Faced
    with the loss of you, I will color
the air about my nose by waving
petals before my eyes, by saying *tomorrow*,
and passing my tongue over puckered lips.

NOTES

"Descent" owes a debt to Naomi Shihab Nye, who said, "No place is exempt from poetry."

For further information about Deccan Volcanism as a possible explanation of the Cretaceous-Tertiary extinction, please see Bianca Bosker's article about Princeton geologist Gerta Keller: "The Nastiest Feud in Science," in the September 2018 issue of *The Atlantic*.

"Ceremony" refers to ears of wheat, which have been used in wedding ceremonies dating back to Roman antiquity, and likely figured into the kind of nuptial feast Shakespeare imagined for the three pairs of lovers in *A Midsummer Night's Dream.*

ACKNOWLEDGMENTS

Grateful acknowledgement is made to the following publications, in which these poems first appeared, sometimes in different forms:

Chaffin Journal: Capsized
Eclectica: Declaring Victory
ghoti: Swamp Walking
Heirlock Magazine: On County H, Near Wabeno, Wisconsin
Indianapolis Review: The Wisdom of Hanna & Barbera
Jenny: The Frog Prince of Wisconsin
Kissing Dynamite: Defense
Lily Poetry Review: Dry Spell
Linden Avenue: The Body
Ponder Review: A Change in the Weather; Devotional
Potpourri: Give Me
RHINO: Roux
Rockvale Review: Hacksaw
SHANTIH: At the Neatline
Stickman Review: Child's Play
Swamp Ape Review: The Theory of Deccan Volcanism
The Texas Poetry Calendar 2021: Running
The Texas Poetry Calendar 2022: Not Going to the Beach
The Texas Poetry Calendar 2023: Matins
Valparaiso Poetry Review: Keeping Time
VOX: Sanctuary

Some of these poems appeared (sometimes in different forms) in the Anchor & Plume Press chapbook *A Hole in the Light* (2015) and in the Seven Kitchens Press chapbook *Wishes Wished Just Hard Enough* (2019).

"Declaring Victory" was reprinted in the anthology *Eclectica Magazine: Best Poetry, Celebrating 20 Years Online* (Eclectica Press, 2016).

Thanks as always to my family both for supporting the work I'm doing now and for making me a reader and writer in the first place. As a kid, I thought it was normal to have framed broadsides on every wall and poetry collections on every surface, and to go with my friends from afternoons of football and street hockey to biweekly book club meetings. I still think it should be.

Thanks to the best friends I could ask for, from Oak Park, Northfield, Philadelphia, Carlisle, Lancaster, Alexandria, D.C., Budapest, Fort Worth, Indianapolis, San Diego, and every stop along the way.

I am more thankful than I can say to the team at Next Page Press. Cathlin and Sheila have provided feedback and support from the start; Judy and Tina brought fresh eyes and ears; Amber has built a beautiful physical artifact. Laura's vision, leadership, and focus have made this project a pure pleasure and have made NPP into both a welcoming home and a literary force.

I am humbled by the time and attention Toby Olson, Octavio Quintanilla, and Lauren Berry Shellberg gave to the manuscript, to say nothing of the generous words with which they have graced the cover of the book. Their work inspires me at every turn.

Madison, this book began to take shape during the first pandemic year, which started mere months after our wedding. I could not have been locked down in a more supportive and loving home.

ABOUT THE AUTHOR

Lucas Jacob is the author of the poetry collection *The Seed Vault* (Eyewear Publishing, 2019) and the chapbooks *A Hole in the Light* (Anchor & Plume Press, 2015) and *Wishes Wished Just Hard Enough* (Seven Kitchens Press, 2019). His poetry and prose have appeared in literary magazines including *Southwest Review*, *Indianapolis Review*, and *RHINO* and in trade journals including *Education Week*, *Independent Teacher*, and the *Journal of Media Literacy*. His career in K–12 education has brought him many wonderful things, including the honor of serving as a Fulbright Fellow in Budapest, Hungary. He is currently the Director of Writing, Communication, and Media Literacy at La Jolla Country Day School, in San Diego.

www.ingramcontent.com/pod-product-compliance
Lightning Source LLC
Chambersburg PA
CBHW030309100526
44590CB00012B/572